THE ART OF FLORENCE

30 Postcards

PRINCIPAL PHOTOGRAPHY BY TAKASHI OKAMURA

◆

ABBEVILLE PRESS • PUBLISHERS
NEW YORK • LONDON • PARIS

Fra Filippo Lippi, *Annunciation*, c. 1440.
Tempera on panel. Martelli Chapel, San Lorenzo.
From *The Art of Florence*, available from Abbeville Press.

ABBEVILLE PUBLISHING GROUP
488 Madison Avenue • New York, NY 10022

SINCE THE RADIANT YEARS OF THE RENAISSANCE, THE CITY OF FLORENCE HAS COME TO REPRESENT THE GREATEST TRIUMPH OF WESTERN CULTURAL TRADITION. THIS IS THE CITY WHERE HUMANISM WAS BORN, WHERE MEN AND WOMEN FIRST FOUND THEMSELVES TO BE THE MEASURE OF ALL THINGS. FOR MORE THAN THREE CENTURIES FLORENCE NURTURED A CREATIVE COMMUNITY OF ASTOUNDING, EVEN REVOLUTIONARY GENIUS. HERE HUNDREDS OF THE MOST SPLENDIDLY TALENTED ARTISTS IN HISTORY LIVED AND WORKED, DRAWING THE WORLD TOWARD A RADICAL NEW VISION OF REALISM AND USHERING IN THE DAZZLING ERA OF THE HIGH RENAISSANCE.

THESE THIRTY SPECTACULAR IMAGES—REPRODUCED WITH A METICULOUS CARE WORTHY OF THE RENAISSANCE CRAFT TRADITION—IMMERSE US IN A RICH PANOPLY OF HUMAN CREATIVITY. THE POWER OF MICHELANGELO'S DAVID, THE BRILLIANCE OF A DA VINCI OR A BOTTICELLI ANNUNCIATION, THE DELICACY OF A FRA ANGELICO ANGEL, THE SPECTACULAR BEAUTY OF A RAPHAEL MADONNA—EACH IMAGE IN THIS LUXURIOUS VISUAL DOCUMENTATION CAPTURES THE MAGICAL ART OF THIS INCOMPARABLE CITY.

Sandro Botticelli, *Primavera*, c. 1482.
Detail: Three Graces.
Tempera on panel. Galleria degli Uffizi.
From *The Art of Florence*, available from Abbeville Press.

ABBEVILLE PUBLISHING GROUP
488 Madison Avenue • New York, NY 10022

MCCCC
LXXXV
ENSE CADENS SOLYMO POMPEI PVLVI
AVGVR
NVMEN AIT QVAE ME CONTEG
VRNA DABIT

Domenico Ghirlandaio, *Adoration of the Shepherds*, 1485.
Tempera on panel. Sassetti Chapel, Santa Trinita.
From *The Art of Florence*, available from Abbeville Press.

ABBEVILLE PUBLISHING GROUP
488 Madison Avenue • New York, NY 10022

Jacopo Pontormo, *Annunciation*, 1527–28.
Detail: Angel.
Fresco. Capponi Chapel, Santa Felicita.
From *The Art of Florence*, available from Abbeville Press.

ABBEVILLE PUBLISHING GROUP
488 Madison Avenue • New York, NY 10022

Gentile da Fabriano, *Adoration of the Magi*, 1423.
Detail of central panel: Worshipping Magi.
Tempera on panel. Galleria degli Uffizi.
From *The Art of Florence*, available from Abbeville Press.

ABBEVILLE PUBLISHING GROUP
488 Madison Avenue • New York, NY 10022

Raffaello Sanzio (Raphael), *Madonna del Granduca*, c. 1505.
Oil on panel. Galleria Palatina, Palazzo Pitti.
From *The Art of Florence*, available from Abbeville Press.

ABBEVILLE PUBLISHING GROUP
488 Madison Avenue • New York, NY 10022

Agnolo Bronzino, *Trinity with Saints Michael, Anthony, Francis, Jerome, and John the Evangelist*, 1540–46.
Fresco. Chapel of Eleonora of Toledo, Palazzo Vecchio.
From *The Art of Florence*, available from Abbeville Press.

ABBEVILLE PUBLISHING GROUP
488 Madison Avenue • New York, NY 10022

Benozzo Gozzoli, *Journey of the Magi, Procession of the Old King,*
1459–61. Detail: Young man.
Fresco. Chapel, Palazzo Medici-Riccardi.
From *The Art of Florence*, available from Abbeville Press.

ABBEVILLE PUBLISHING GROUP
488 Madison Avenue • New York, NY 10022

Fra Filippo Lippi, *Annunciation*, c. 1440.
Tempera on panel. Martelli Chapel, San Lorenzo.
From *The Art of Florence*, available from Abbeville Press.

ABBEVILLE PUBLISHING GROUP
488 Madison Avenue • New York, NY 10022

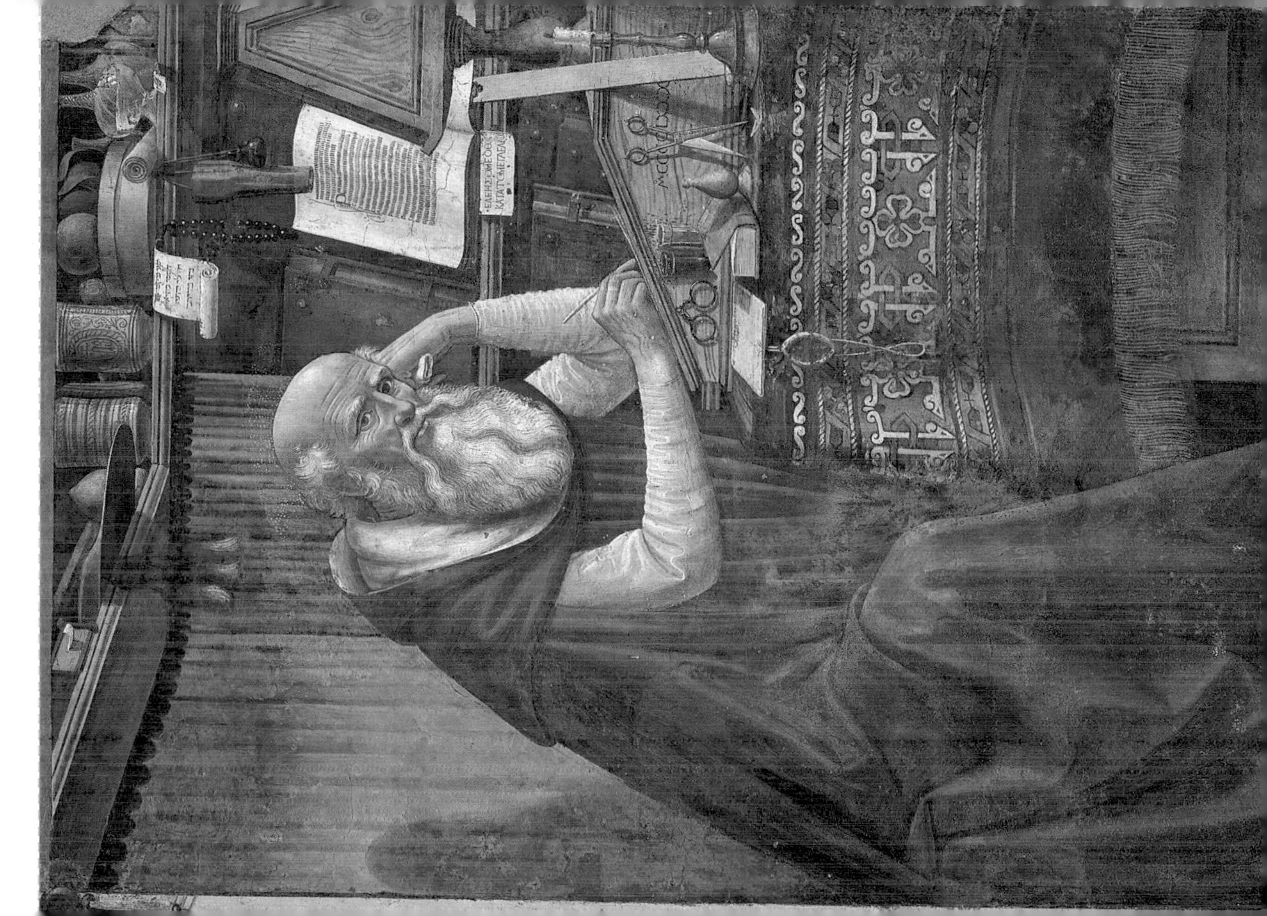

Domenico Ghirlandaio, *Saint Jerome in His Study*, 1480.
Fresco. Ognissanti.
From *The Art of Florence*, available from Abbeville Press.

ABBEVILLE PUBLISHING GROUP
488 Madison Avenue • New York, NY 10022

Fra Angelico, *Last Judgment*, early 1430s.
Detail: The Blessed.
Tempera on panel. Museo di San Marco.
From *The Art of Florence*, available from Abbeville Press.

ABBEVILLE PUBLISHING GROUP
488 Madison Avenue • New York, NY 10022

Leonardo da Vinci and others, *Annunciation*, 1472–75.
Detail: The Angel Gabriel.
Oil on panel. Galleria degli Uffizi.
From *The Art of Florence*, available from Abbeville Press.

ABBEVILLE PUBLISHING GROUP
488 Madison Avenue • New York, NY 10022

Raffaello Sanzio (Raphael), *Maddalena Doni*, 1505–7.
Oil on panel. Galleria Palatina, Palazzo Pitti.
From *The Art of Florence*, available from Abbeville Press.

ABBEVILLE PUBLISHING GROUP
488 Madison Avenue • New York, NY 10022

Jacopo Pontormo, *Entombment/Deposition*, 1525–26.
Oil on panel. Capponi Chapel, Santa Felicita.
From *The Art of Florence*, available from Abbeville Press.

ABBEVILLE PUBLISHING GROUP
488 Madison Avenue • New York, NY 10022

Michelangelo Buonarroti, *Doni Holy Family*, c. 1504–6.
Tempera on panel. Galleria degli Uffizi.
From *The Art of Florence*, available from Abbeville Press.

ABBEVILLE PUBLISHING GROUP
488 Madison Avenue • New York, NY 10022

Michelangelo Buonarroti, *Madonna of the Steps*, c. 1490–92.
Marble. Casa Buonarroti.
From *The Art of Florence*, available from Abbeville Press.

ABBEVILLE PUBLISHING GROUP
488 Madison Avenue • New York, NY 10022

Rinuccini Master, *Rinuccini Triptych*, third quarter of 14th century.
Central panel: *Apparition of the Virgin to Saint Bernard.*
Tempera on panel. Galleria dell'Accademia.
From *The Art of Florence*, available from Abbeville Press.

ABBEVILLE PUBLISHING GROUP
488 Madison Avenue • New York, NY 10022

Domenico Veneziano, *Madonna and Child*, c. 1440.
Tempera on panel. Villa I Tatti, Settignano.
From *The Art of Florence*, available from Abbeville Press.

ABBEVILLE PUBLISHING GROUP
488 Madison Avenue • New York, NY 10022

Sandro Botticelli, *Birth of Venus*, c. 1485.
Detail: Zephyr and a nymph.
Tempera on canvas. Galleria degli Uffizi.
From *The Art of Florence*, available from Abbeville Press.

ABBEVILLE PUBLISHING GROUP
488 Madison Avenue • New York, NY 10022

Fra Angelico and workshop, *Mocking of Christ*, late 1430s–early 1440s.
Detail: Dominic in contemplation.
Fresco. Monastery of San Marco.
From *The Art of Florence*, available from Abbeville Press.

ABBEVILLE PUBLISHING GROUP
488 Madison Avenue • New York, NY 10022

Andrea del Verrocchio and Leonardo da Vinci, *Baptism of Christ*, early to mid-1470s. Detail: Angels.
Tempera and oil on panel. Galleria degli Uffizi.
From *The Art of Florence*, available from Abbeville Press.

ABBEVILLE PUBLISHING GROUP
488 Madison Avenue • New York, NY 10022

Fra Filippo Lippi, *Madonna and Child*, c. 1465.
Tempera on panel. Galleria degli Uffizi.
From *The Art of Florence*, available from Abbeville Press.

ABBEVILLE PUBLISHING GROUP
488 Madison Avenue • New York, NY 10022

Masaccio, *Trinity*, c. 1425.
Fresco. Santa Maria Novella.
From *The Art of Florence*, available from Abbeville Press.

ABBEVILLE PUBLISHING GROUP
488 Madison Avenue • New York, NY 10022

Michelangelo Buonarroti, *David*, 1501–3.
Detail: Right profile.
Marble. Galleria dell'Accademia.
From *The Art of Florence*, available from Abbeville Press.

ABBEVILLE PUBLISHING GROUP
488 Madison Avenue • New York, NY 10022

Raffaello Sanzio (Raphael), *Agnolo Doni*, 1505–7.
Oil on panel. Galleria Palatina, Palazzo Pitti.
From *The Art of Florence*, available from Abbeville Press.

ABBEVILLE PUBLISHING GROUP
488 Madison Avenue • New York, NY 10022

Workshop of Fra Angelico, *Madonna della Stella*, 1435.
Tempera on panel. Museo di San Marco.
From *The Art of Florence*, available from Abbeville Press.

ABBEVILLE PUBLISHING GROUP
488 Madison Avenue • New York, NY 10022

Fra Angelico, *Naming of the Baptist*, c. 1434–35.
Tempera on panel. Museo di San Marco.
From *The Art of Florence*, available from Abbeville Press.

ABBEVILLE PUBLISHING GROUP
488 Madison Avenue • New York, NY 10022

Agnolo Bronzino, *Eleonora of Toledo and Giovanni de' Medici*, c. 1544–45.
Tempera on panel. Galleria degli Uffizi.
From *The Art of Florence*, available from Abbeville Press.

ABBEVILLE PUBLISHING GROUP
488 Madison Avenue • New York, NY 10022

Jacopo Pontormo, *Annunciation*, 1527–28.
Detail: Virgin.
Fresco. Capponi Chapel, Santa Felicita.
From *The Art of Florence*, available from Abbeville Press.

ABBEVILLE PUBLISHING GROUP
488 Madison Avenue • New York, NY 10022

Benozzo Gozzoli, *Journey of the Magi, Procession of the Moorish King*, 1459–61. Detail: King (Byzantine Emperor John VIII Paleologus). Fresco. Chapel, Palazzo Medici-Riccardi.
From *The Art of Florence*, available from Abbeville Press.

ABBEVILLE PUBLISHING GROUP
488 Madison Avenue • New York, NY 10022

Sandro Botticelli, *Annunciation*, 1489–90.
Tempera on panel. Galleria degli Uffizi.
From *The Art of Florence*, available from Abbeville Press.

ABBEVILLE PUBLISHING GROUP
488 Madison Avenue • New York, NY 10022